A LIFE MORE TRAVELLED

From Fear To Adventure...

by Jo Warwick

ISBN: 978-0-9956607-2-4

Published in the United Kingdom

Cover Design by CRJ Design

Editing by Victoria Haslan

www.jowarwick.com

To Faith With Love Forever

"Follow your bliss.

If you follow your bliss,

you put yourself on a kind of track

that has been there all the while waiting for you,

and the life you ought to be living is the one you are living.

When you can see that, you begin to meet people

who are in the field of your bliss, and they open the doors to you.

I say, follow your bliss and don't be afraid,

and doors will open where you didn't know they were going to be.

If you follow your bliss,

doors will open for you that wouldn't have opened for anyone else."

— **Joseph Campbell**

Table of Contents

About Jo Warwick

Jo lives by the sea in Cornwall, UK. A former professional sportswoman, born spiritual energy healer, turned therapist and psychologist (individuals, couples, children and family), she specialised in human development, attachment and Love. She has worked with thousands of men and women in the UK, Ireland, Europe, USA, Canada and Australia, to heal wounds on love, life and embrace their empowerment and skills to living life their way — in alignment with their joy, happiness and the Law of Attraction.

Now she follows her passion as a writer and speaker. For six years she previously wrote for a number of personal development and inspirational sites, as well as contributing to other books, magazines and professional therapeutic journals. Writing and language has been a life long passion and in 2016 she published her first book 'The Big Book Of Love - Loving Yourself, Dating With Love, Loving Relationships'. Combining her professional and personal experience and storytelling, with the inspired guidance she has shared with clients all over the world and uses herself.

Her passion for global travelling is not just to explore different cultures and environments, but for the love of new people, new experiences and self discovery. All of which has been the foundation to her own personal growth and an inspiration for her writing. **www.jowarwick.com**

Introduction

To travel is a surface experience of getting from A to B, whereas travelling is about immersing in the experience. Immersing in the journey of where we are each moment, and the new places to come. We may not always be physically moving, or moving far, but we are moving internally, and in our senses, as we flow with the experience of living.

Travelling is a journey of exploration into the wider world and an internal journey within. It offers a chance to step out of the familiar and into new surroundings, to widen your mind and experience yourself and the world around you in wholly new ways.

It allows for easily uncovering fears, beliefs and resistance that may be holding us back in our day to day life, and the opportunity to set them free as we boldly, or sometimes with trepidation, step forward and gain confidence in our own capabilities.

To know oneself is to know others and the world, but we cannot always see ourselves in the familiar, as our focus becomes fixated on what we see and know, and how people respond to us.

Instead of how we feel and what gives us most joy as we move towards it.

The curious thing about travelling the globe is that the focus is all about oneself. We see things we like and dislike, but it is our personal experience that fascinates us and whether we wish to continue to see more of it or less. To know who we are and what rocks our world internally, so that when we return to the familiarity of home, we can take with us our open mind and new awareness to alter, create and expand our ways of living, so that it resonates and fits with what feels so good to our unique self.

Life is an ongoing journey externally and internally. Where we learn to grow, create and expand in who we are and who we share our lives with and what we enjoy doing. It is this full permission of travelling physically that helps us to get more capable in our skill of self-discovery and the tools for getting the most out of each journey.

Travelling anywhere can help you to live more fully. You don't have to go far and physically travel hundreds of miles, but you do need to step out of the familiarity of your surroundings to experience the joy of difference and contrast to uncover what rocks your world as an individual. You need to acknowledge that although we can share our journey with others it always remains an individual and personal experience.

I have used the wider world as a playground, an experiment, a place to run to and away from at different times. In this book, I will share what I have discovered and translated to daily living. Using personal anecdotes, I will guide you through the skills to embrace the bigger journey of life and step out of fear and move into its wondrous adventure of enjoyment, fun, exploration and connection.

The background for these stories are from my experiences further afield in Asia, USA, South Africa, France, Italy, Holland and closer to home from a three-month meandering road trip around the UK. Although there are many other places and times I could have shared these are the ones that wanted to be written.

There is so much more of the world I want to explore and so much more of myself to discover. Neither adventure will ever be complete, but these core understandings and wisdoms of living may help you, as they have helped me, to be braver, bolder and explore for yourself. To follow your bliss out of fear and into the adventure and joy of being alive every day.

I hope that my musings on life and the adventures that took me there, inspire you to see your experience of living as an adventure, and that we are travelling in a world which is abundant with amazing things to see, feel and taste and many wonderful, interesting, diverse people to meet - it is all there just waiting for you if you wish to choose it.

Chapter 1: Keep All Baggage to a Minimum

When it comes to any form of travelling, anything you take, you must carry. The more you think you need to pack and hold onto, the heavier it's going to be to carry.

Like many young people, I went backpacking for the first time in Australia. I set off prepared for every eventuality. My backpack was huge, heavy and cumbersome to manoeuvre. Not only were my muscles aching and my skin chaffed but it was draining the fun from my experience.

Travelling is supposed to be about freedom and living spontaneously in the moment but I was severely hindered, as everywhere I went I had to lug around this giant inconvenience. When I did occasionally find somewhere to store it, I felt totally paranoid that I would lose everything, so attached had I become to my stuff. Eventually I was forced to let go and make changes.

During a visit to the public toilets in Sydney Harbour, I'd negotiated getting my bag off to get into the small cubicle. However, when I stepped out into the wash area the weight of returning it onto my back made me fall backwards. Just like that, I was an upturned beetle stuck on its back, my legs and arms flailing around.

I couldn't budge, either to the side or forward. I was stuck, immovable. With my shoulders pinned down, I couldn't release the strap at my waist fastening me to my backpack. I could do nothing but stay marooned on the bathroom floor until someone found me. Thankfully it was a busy spot, because in the end it took three people to help me get up and going again!

After this incident, I sat down in the sun and gutted my bag. I was only a few weeks into my trip, but I'd had enough. I threw anything I hadn't used up to that point into the nearest bin.

Keep all baggage to a minimum; that's a definite rule for life. The more baggage you carry the more energy you waste. That goes for both physical and emotional baggage. To enjoy the journey of life and get the most out of it, we need to be able to move freely and be light enough to be spontaneous, adaptable and playful.

Don't end up stuck like me, waiting for someone to rescue you. Be aware of your 'carry-on weight, just as you would if you were boarding a flight! Every so often rummage through your life, enjoy having a good clear out and letting go of what is not really needed.

When it comes to material stuff, I tend to go with the rule that if I haven't used it for a year or two I will chuck it out, pass it on or give it to charity, unless it has sentimental value.

Physical baggage, such as excess fat in our bodies can have the same effect; slowing our journey through life, but also our ability to adapt to new experiences. As conscious as we are of what we are putting in our suitcases or backpacks, it's important to check out what food we are putting in our bodies. For me, consuming sugar played a big part in weighing me down – mentally, emotionally and physically – and I finally realised the problem, bit the bullet, and changed my diet for good (with a little coaching help to re-educate me).

With emotional baggage, it can seem a little harder, although all you need is to give yourself a little attention, connect with those suppressed feelings and express yourself. Do whatever it takes to let it go, forgive and pack up what you are happy to carry and get on with living.

A word of warning though, be careful not to "throw the baby out with the bath water". I went on an important three day business trip to Rome a few years later and I was so proud of my efficient packing but when I unpacked in the hotel I discovered I hadn't packed any shoes. I was wearing trainers which didn't quite match the dress-suit I had packed. Of course, I made the best of bad situation and went shopping. Not a bad city to buy shoes in!

As we travel through life we make beautiful memories and experiences that create wisdom and the tools for living; keep hold and revisit them because these make up your core travel kit.

Be aware of the essentials; let go of everything else...

Chapter 2: It's Not A Picture

While visiting Amsterdam, I met a guy in his early twenties on the tourist boat. He was far from home and travelling alone, but not for the first time. As we sat on the hop on and off tourist boat that floats around the city canals, he explained he'd spent the whole of the day before travelling around on the tourist bus. He made it clear he had no intention of getting off anywhere. He hadn't the day before and wouldn't today. He intended to just sit, watch the city go by and listen to the audio descriptions. Then he would leave the following day, onto another European city.

This is not travelling. He was simply observing the world, like watching TV. To experience life we have to get stuck in, feel the moment and use our senses.

While he sat, I got off the boat at the famous Amsterdam Art Museum to admire Rembrandts, Van Goghs, and work by other masters of art, all of whom had given so much passion and energy to their creations. I paused here and there to sit on the viewing seats to have a fuller perspective, pay my attention to these enormous pieces and allow myself to be affected by them. I was met by streams of people walking up close to the picture, taking a photo of it on their phone and immediately moving on. They seemed oblivious to everything and everyone around them. I'm not even sure they knew you could sit and simply admire.

It was hilarious and a bit sad to watch. They were blind to the detail, the shifts in perspective, its emotional impact and the subjectivity of art. We can dislike it, be blown away, or just indifferent, but we cannot know our response while we are detached, rushing and only observing. Art, like life, is intimate and personal and if beauty is in the eye of the beholder, without a beholder there is nothing.

When travelling, I seek to engage with each new location, the people, the smells, the food, the sights and how I respond to them; without this I might as well be reading a travel guide from the comfort of my sofa. It would be a waste of my time, energy, money and life – and I'm not prepared to do that.

Guides are great but they're there to whet your appetite and assist in creating action. The journey of life is one way – there is only one moment of experiencing a place for the first time. That never comes again. It is the opportunity and magic of now. We can always revisit, which can be fun too, but it will always be a different experience.

The young lad in Amsterdam was scared and letting his fear hold him back from actually exploring. He was already there – he had done the hard bit of getting on the plane, now he just had to play and enjoy himself!

We are already alive, grown up and have got this far – we might as well do our best to be present in the journey and enjoy living each moment in the amazing world we are visiting. It will be over soon enough.

Chapter 3: When You're Feeling Lost

There is no such thing, really, as getting lost. This sounds strange because when you don't know where you are or where you're going, it is instilled in you to think that you're lost.

We're not lost – we're simply going around in circles getting disorientated, as I found out while running early one morning in the middle of central France with my dog.

As I set out on my first epic road trip through Europe, one of my biggest fears was getting lost. How could I get lost when I didn't have a fixed destination or itinerary? I discovered my fear was actually whether I could trust myself; if I end up in the wrong place, can I find my way out?

As it was summer, I had set off early in the morning to get the coolest part of the day. I had done a little investigation with a map the evening before to make sure I knew where I was going. I was certain I was well prepared.

I had my headphones on – I was singing along to music, running in the beautiful countryside and feeling very happy with myself. Suddenly, I realised I didn't recognise anything around me. I had stopped paying attention to where I was going. "Thats OK," I thought, "I'll just go back the way I came," but as I started running back, I had a sinking feeling. I still didn't recognise anything – it was as though someone had spun me around and changed the landscape. Had I turned the wrong direction without realising it?

My phone had no signal, houses were sparse and it was still so early in the morning there were little to no people to ask. Those I did meet either didn't stop to help, or became hindered by colloquial language and misunderstanding. I would set off in fits and spurts following pointed fingers and gestures, their directions making me steadily more confused.

Panic began to rise as I felt more and more frustrated. Eventually I found myself standing in the middle of a crossroads surrounded by nothing but fields.

Overwhelmed and scared, I felt like my worst fear was coming true. I had no idea where the campsite was, along with my tent, car and belongings. I couldn't find help and I had made the rookie mistake of not bringing water. The day was getting hotter and hotter and I was worried about my dog, Faith.

In the end, so frustrated and getting more panicky, I jumped up and down on the spot shouting, swearing, screaming, crying at the universe, until I surrendered to how things were. Now a bit more clear minded I set off in search of a tree to go sit in the shade of the leaves, cool down and take some deep breaths, to calm down.

While sitting under the tree, gradually becoming more relaxed, I saw a farmhouse near by. I then remembered there was a large water tower that stood near to the campsite, which I needed to aim for.

I got myself together and headed off to the farm to be greeted by a welcoming woman who spoke a little more English than the people I had encountered so far. After giving Faith and I some water, she pointed me in the right direction.

I had only been 10 minutes away this whole time. I had been going around literally in a circle, unable to see the obvious sign I was looking for.

To get the most out of life we have to be curious and explore, but on the way we will need to be able to conquer our fears. I've found that theses six essentials keep me going and moving forward.

1. Always prepare as much as you can with your essentials but sometimes you have to just go do it.

2. Do your best to be present and aware in the moment.

3. If you lose your way try not to panic.

4. If you are panicking, let out the intensity of emotions and take some time to relax. This will help you become receptive to the solution.

5. Get clear about what you will need to solve your problem.

6. Don't be afraid to continue asking for help until you get what you need.

Chapter 4: When Opportunity Comes …

Eight years ago, I was contacted out of the blue by my dear friend Liz and offered a free holiday with her to Koh Samui, leaving the next day. All I had to do was get myself from Cornwall to London before the flight the following evening. The timing was incredible. I was breaking up from my part-time counselling job for the Easter school holidays, so after sorting private clients and someone to feed the cats I was good to go.

Everything fell into to place with ease, like a huge open door. All I had to do was walk through. Then I got scared. I had never been to Asia, although it was on my bucket list. When I'm travelling I find it easy to change plans, go with the flow and follow inspiration and opportunities as they show up. However I admit I had got a little stuck – stuck in routine, working too hard and in a personal situation at home. I was in need of some distance and perspective and here I was with the good fortune of being offered exactly what I needed to give me that.

Insane fears rattled around my brain trying to battle excitement, until my mum asked one simple question: "How would you feel if you didn't go...?" It was simple – I would be gutted and I knew instantly it would be the wrong decision not to go. How could I miss out on such an amazing experience and shun this obvious gift horse?

So I took a deep breath and got on with packing. By the next evening I was sitting on the overnight plane to Bangkok in spacious bulk-head seats between a handsome music producer and my dear friend.

Not every opportunity is so clear-cut and sometimes things are sign posts to where you want to go next – little inspirations to direct you. Whether it's a big leap or just a shift in direction when these doors open there is only one choice: look forward and say yes.

In that moment we are being offered the chance to shake it all up, grow and step out of our known zone – even if it isn't so comfortable – and into the great wide unknown of opportunity. So in this case being a bit scared is a very good sign!

This leap through the open door into the unknown brought me sunshine, relaxation, incredible food, culture, playing with elephants, outstanding tropical beauty, swimming in lagoons. It gave me the chance to change my narrow perspective and recharge my batteries, so I could see a solution and way forward with my life at home.

Above all I got the experience of unforgettable quality time, sharing an adventure, creating memories and endless conversations with a very dear friend through her immense generosity.

JO WARWICK

Chapter 5: The Signs That Guide You

One of the greatest things I've learned from travelling is that there are always sign posts pointing to where you need to go. The more we become aware of these little nudges and drops of information, the more we can relax and move along the stepping stones of our journey with ease. Ignore them, and things become more and more of a struggle, as I was forcefully reminded while on a three-month trip exploring the UK.

Having always travelled further afield, I decided to spend some time exploring my own country. I was mesmerised by its beauty and vast diversity of landscape. However my heart was stolen by the Lake District. The vivid colours, lush hills and mountains, deep blue lakes and rivers – it was like being in Switzerland.

After two weeks of bliss I thought I'd better move on. I had a BS belief that I mustn't have too much of a good thing and my tendency was to respond by upping sticks and starting again. There is a place for shaking things up but, as this experience showed me, if you love somewhere and you don't have to leave, all it could take is a tweak here and there for it to continue to be great.

I decided to drive from west to east across the north of the UK. Leaving the western Lake District, which sits on the coastline of Cumbria, I began driving towards the striking, yet contrasting, desolate Yorkshire Dales to fight with the heavy traffic at Scotch Corner.

Driving away from the Lake District I began to feel a sense of foreboding, but brushed it away as silliness. As the traffic got more congested my engine warning light suddenly came on, so I pulled into the first farm entrance I could find to assess the situation. During the five minutes it took to check with my car manual, my engine light disappeared and another car had appeared and blocked me in — which I only discovered when I reversed straight into it. It was a bright red Alfa Romeo! Amazingly there was no damage to either car, to which the other driver proclaimed it was a miracle!

Blindly and stubbornly, I continued on my journey. Having spent the past two weeks at a gentle pace, relaxing and lightheartedly chatting to those I met, I now spent hours and hours stop-starting in thick traffic. I was surrounded by grumpy people, of which I was gradually becoming one of. I tried to improve my mindset, by stopping at the only café I could find to take a break, only to be told they had stopped serving.

I finally arrived at my new campsite to be greeted by not only a cold climate, but a cold and unwelcoming woman. My stomach sank. I knew I had made a mistake, but again brushed it off and hoped it would all be better in the morning.

Exhausted, I put my tent up and settled down for the evening. After ignoring my intuition, it was as if the night ahead was determined to make sure I got the message. I would get no sleep due to the endless barking from the local hounds next door, who in turn set off the geese or vice versa, which was eventually topped off by a cacophony of noise with the dawn chorus of the whole farmyard for two hours. If that wasn't enough to seal the deal, I'm not sure I have ever been so cold!

I packed up and went to speak to the owner, politely explaining that I would be changing my plans, having originally booked to stay for six nights. It only confirmed my decision when she went on to childishly sulk, ignore me and withhold a refund.

This kind of intense experience has happened three times in my travels, and I have played it out many, many times in my day-to-day life – the outcomes have differed depending on whether I've been stubborn or if I have followed my instincts.

Sometimes I forget and then I have an experience that reminds me to be more aware and trust in myself and the signs presented. What I've learnt is that being on the right path feels like being in the warm sunshine, and unfolds and increases with playful enjoyment. Whereas the wrong path is like falling off the stepping stone into cold water and gets more and more uncomfortable with time.

I have explored and described more about this navigation system for a successful and joyful life in The Big Book of Love.

Chapter 6: Weighing Up The Risks

Every adventure has risk, because it is the potential of risk that makes life exciting.

In my late twenties I spent some time travelling around central South Africa on a conservation project redistributing wild animals to different farms and parks for population growth and stability. Although this was my fourth trip to South Africa, this was a massive step out of my comfort zone.

The climate of the country was very different at that time, although it had improved since my earlier trips. On the surface this trip was filled with a vast amount of risk, from the political and social flux of the country at the time to the diversity of cultural beliefs that caused friction and health risks. Racism, sexism, ageism and every other prejudice you could imagine was clear in this divided country, and judgement was rife. However it was always unstable and there was consistency in the instability,

It sounds like madness, but in reality it was easy to focus on my own wellbeing, trust my instinct and hangout with the people I felt comfortable and safe with. Realistically, our greatest danger was in the wild as our group of 15 spent most of our time in the remote plains, just like you see on TV, with barely a bush to have a pee behind.

On one assignment we had to capture, sedate and relocate two hundred springbok. Having been tracked and monitored using a light helicopter, they were then driven into a giant funnel made up of giant green canvas curtains.

We only had a brief window of opportunity to capture and sedate them as the stress can cause them to die. Speed was of the essence, so it was our job to be efficient as possible. The problem with springbok is that not only are they fast, but as their name suggests, they jump really high and their hoofs are as sharp as razor blades – they can cut swiftly and deeply into skin.

We had to jump and rugby tackle them around the belly, avoiding the hooves, pin them to the ground, swiftly grab their legs and tie them together. They were then given anti-stress medication so they were asleep for the trip. To be as considerate as possible, we needed to be firm and swift.

It was like the weirdest and riskiest game of British Bulldog, as we stood to be rushed by our opponents. We faced these elegant, wild, golden beasts as they bounced and dashed past like Tigger on speed.

Risk ran through the whole trip from beginning to end but only at one point did I ever worry about my physical safety. Our car broke down at night on a notoriously dangerous road not just for bad drivers, but for attacks, but it was soon resolved and we were fine.

I could not know any of this in advance, I just had to take the risk of entering something completely unknown. What I got in return was memories of being so close to truly wild mammals, including lion cubs, that I could smell, touch and see them in all their glory, instead of just on TV. I watched the enormous, bright orange sun fall out of the sky every night over the vast, dusty horizon and heard how noisy the wilderness can actually be. I lay on the dusty earth gazing at the millions of stars in the Milky Way and tripped out on how clear and close they seemed. I stood on the back of a pickup truck going 80mph across the plain, and got close to a wild rhino in the dark.

It wasn't all wild and dramatic – there were many long periods of waiting, playing cards, laying in the warm African sun, dancing to the car radio in the middle of nowhere, simply hanging out and wasting time, and lots of preparation, cleaning, sorting and mending. I made friends and saw a very different way of life. I had fascinating and sometimes odd conversations. Most of all I got to connect with the beauty of South Africa away from the more populated or developed areas.

Every risk was worth it to have all these experiences. Risk doesn't always have to be as wild, but there's only one question we can ask ourselves when faced with an opportunity. Whether it's letting go to love, exploring a new career, following a passion, buying a house or heading off on an adventure in the wider world all we can ask is, "Do I feel the risk is worth it?"

Chapter 7: Mistakes

For someone so bold, it is important that I share one of my biggest fears and how I have learnt from it.

I suffered a serious horse riding accident in my early twenties which stopped my professional equestrian career. I made a mistake that injured my leg so badly I needed three operations to recover. In time, I healed physically and fought my way back to riding, but inside I was left with a deep insidious fear of being hurt that I've had to battle every time I stepped out to do anything new.

This fear used to penetrate my relationships, hindered me from following my passions and dreams, and kept me from truly giving myself. Not for fear of others hurting me, but that I would hurt myself by making a mistake or the wrong choice.

This confused belief manifested as a self-fulfilling prophecy until I became almost paralysed – this time not physically, but mentally.

I stood safely on the side-lines, trying to protect myself, but instead was hurting myself by missing out on the experiences and opportunities for me to grow, to love, and to receive recognition and success.

I have not learnt how to kill this fear, because a little fear is healthy to keep us alert, I have learnt though how to see it for what it really is, to know how to control it, work with it and not feed it.

A time came when I decided I had to face my fears head on and began a three-month journey where I would walk alone around Italy and France.

No planning, no safety nets. I would trust in life, relish the challenge of exploring and commit to every moment. Instead of standing on the sidelines, I gave myself fully to the experience, to what I was doing and what I saw, heard, smelled, tasted and felt with no expectations, just curiosity. Some of those experiences, people and places were stunning or extraordinary and others were ugly and disappointing, but they were all experiences that gave me something to discover about myself.

As the journey went along, I became more confident and braver to explore further afield. I was rewarded with magical moments, like a field of mint with a 1000 multi-coloured butterflies that flew into the air as I walked through it, or being so close to a large wild deer I could nearly touch her.

Whilst I was based in the central French hills, I set off to explore the acres of forest and the pilgrims' path that weaves its way through the region. Feeling buoyant and confident, I strode out at quite a pace with the sun shining on my back, enjoying feeling my muscles working. I followed the wooded trails here and there, at times having to backtrack as the path became overgrown or petered out, but this didn't deter me. I was feeling good.

Four hours later, as I was heading back my foot slipped, my ankle twisted and I heard the scrape of gravel as the rocky path loomed up to meet my face as my hands reached out to meet it. I slid forward, scraping my bare legs on the gravel and ripping the skin on my palms. I was flat out and face down. My skin burned and I felt a little stunned.

I picked myself up slowly, only now noticing that I was on an uneven path on a downwards slope. I found a grassy patch to one side and sat down to survey the damage. A little blood here and there, the odd graze, but overall nothing too bad. My ankle hurt and my skin stung, but not as much as my pride.

So I sat, breathed and let the moment pass, and eventually gave my ankle a wiggle. All that was left was a big grazed cut on my left palm. I was hurt and I felt a little pain but the damage was minimal;

nothing that a bit of antiseptic cream and some all-important TLC wouldn't heal. However this small incident gave me a big opportunity to learn from.

Taking my time, I brushed myself down, picked myself up and renegotiated my footing. I realised that before I'd fallen my mind had been wandering, thinking about work and other things, not looking or focusing on what I was doing. I had been walking at the same powerful pace as I had uphill and on the flat, but the terrain had changed and I hadn't adapted to it. So now I made sure I took slower, steadier steps, concentrating on where I was going and staying present in the moment.

Mistakes happen. This time I didn't berate myself for it. My fear of making a mistake and getting hurt was rooted in shame. Shame for not being perfect, perhaps, but definitely shame for not taking better care of myself all those years ago and resulting in serious injury.

Part of growing our skills in life is knowing we need different tools, skills and awareness for life's different terrain. Going downhill is like living embracing the flow of your soul, passion and joy. We don't need to put in so much effort, we just need to allow the energy and momentum to do the work. If we relax and listen to our intuition, it's easy and effortless at times which is a clear sign that we're on the right path. However it's still essential though to give our full attention to what we are experiencing, so we stay grounded in our bodies. Don't push too hard or we end up losing balance and falling flat on our faces. Lose concentration, and we make mistakes and get hurt!

I've learnt that being open, present and connected to my mind, body and soul means there is no need to be afraid of not getting it right and getting hurt, because I can adapt my behaviour and responses accordingly.

I know I have the resources and the skills to be brave and move forward with one foot in front of the other with my best interests at heart. I can trust that I can take care of myself, even if that means that I occasionally trip or fall. I can brush myself down, pick myself up and get back on with what I was doing and where I was going, because that it the only way to beat fear.

JO WARWICK

Chapter 8: Never Lose Sleep

Sleep and rest can completely alter how we see and approach the world around us and how well we travel through it. I have struggled with getting the balance right in my life. As an active person, it can annoy me when I want to keep living, moving forward and enjoying myself when I'm injured, ill or simply tired. I used to go through a pattern of all or nothing, so I would keep doing until I collapsed, but I've got better at that.

That's not to say I don't love to sleep and dream. I adore a good bed and have slept in a variety of places throughout my life, sometimes more comfortably than others.– four poster beds in chateaus, peoples' spare rooms, boats, giant dorm rooms with bed bugs and lots of snoring, tents with other bugs, five star hotel rooms, roadside motels, royal stately beds with wall paper of gold leaf, famous historic bedrooms, under the stars in the bush, in the back of my car, and everything in between. I've been so cold that I couldn't sleep at all and so hot that I tossed and turned through the sweats and foggy nightmares.

What we all need is the right amount of good natural sleep, somewhere safe, comfortable, right temperature and unhindered by interruption, alcohol or drugs. Without enough I don't like who I become: I become over alert, confused, stressed, easily irritated and these are not the qualities that grease the pole of traveling through life. When I'm no longer comfortable in my skin, it's impossible to enjoy myself, no matter what I'm doing.

Eight years ago, I lost balance once again whilst growing my private practice. I'd not been travelling for a few years and I'd become so focused that I had forgotten to take any kind of holiday either. I thought I was fine, but in truth I had become unaware of myself and was no longer conscious of my behaviour. I was dashing around doing too much of nothing and something until I started making silly mistakes over and over.

I finally came to my senses after a culmination of nudges from the Universe, and finally recognised that I needed to get away and have more than a weekend off. I booked a last minute holiday at the end of October to the Canary Islands. This would be a very different experience for me, as it was an all inclusive package holiday in a hotel. I wasn't going to visit the island, I was going to revisit me. I needed a place where I didn't need to think about food or going out. All I had to do was move from the pool to my room and totally switch off.

By the time I left four days later, my body and brain were going into shut down and the thought of packing, driving to Bristol Airport and parking seemed exhausting but I did it. As soon as I got seated on the plane I was out cold.

A few hours later, I arrived in the warm resort and got into my room. Every thing looked great and the weather was gorgeous. I went to change into my swimming costume and discovered I'd forgotten all of my summer clothes, which were still lying on my spare bed ready to be packed. All I had remembered was my swimmers, underwear. As well as the coat, jumper, jeans and trainers I'd been wearing to travel when I left the cold UK behind. This time my emotional baggage was so heavy, I'd forgotten to carry my necessary physical baggage. Thankfully I'd remembered my swimming costume so I had a swim and promptly passed out under an umbrella in the sun for four hours.

We live in a seemingly fast paced world and with so many possibilities. To get the most out of life and play though it is essential to make time in our day-to-day life to rest, unwind, and sleep. I find meditation can really help, but sometimes we just need to stop doing anything at all, until we are recharged to get going again.

Chapter 9: Always Seek To Play

The general view of avid global travellers is that the planet and everything and everyone in it is one giant beautiful playground to be admired, tasted, explored, appreciated, loved, shared and, above all, experienced.

When we are open to play, we see the fun to be had – whether that be in the country we visit, the city we get lost in, the food we taste, the smells we inhale or the sights we see. People are innately designed to play and a playful attitude allows us to fool around, get out of ourselves, explore, get involved, dispel fear and get stuck into living and connecting with other people, while having a good time in our personal game of life.

To play we must be relaxed and willing, and as like attracts like, the more we play the more relaxed and open to the opportunities of life we become. Richard Branson mentions in his autobiography that when he sees an opportunity in business or a big challenge, so he only goes for it if it excites him and he feels in his gut that it will be fun to do. He plays in everything he does and this attitude has played a huge part in creating his empire, as well as being the foundation to his life-long friendships and family.

Of course, in life and travelling there are always some bumps to navigate, but by seeing them as a fun challenge and an opportunity to be have a playful attitude about it, it can help us to sail over the bumps with ease.

While white water rafting in Australia, I clung to the side of the boat as eight of us bounced our way down through the rapids. We looked truly ridiculous with our white soup bowl hats and orange life vests, but we didn't care as we were propelled out of our seats. The adrenaline was pumping and we were in the excitement and fear of the moment together.

One minute I was laughing in the boat and the next I was swirling around in the white water. As my life vest buoyed me to the surface, I became stuck under the boat and had to bob back down again.

I was briefly scared but the next second I was bobbing up again and hauled out of the water by the others. I felt foolish, but everyone just laughed and patted me on the back, and soon we were back whooping and cheering as we flew out of our seats and then over a small waterfall.

The sun was shining and we were in the boat together. There were no mistakes, no silliness, we were all fools having a good time and our high energy buoyed our journey.

This vibrancy continued to float me along as I got swept up in a flirtation and brief affair with one of the instructors. I was young and he was a gorgeous, fit, tanned, gentle, kind, fun-loving Australian who I will always remember fondly. Playing with the group in the raft was exhilarating, but playing with the guy was intimate, giggly, sexy and made me feel beautiful.

When we play, we stretch our boundaries and our comfort zones. We connect; we laugh; we have good time; we learn by going too far or not far enough; we become braver and discover who we are and what we are truly capable of. Sometimes we make memories that last forever.

This attitude and way of being translates into how we approach the career we follow, the new hobby we want to try, our intimate relationships, the way we approach love or dating, the business we decide to build, the wild adventure to travel the world. The list is endless, because truly it is an attitude for life if you want an abundant and happy one.

The world is one big boat and most people are longing to connect, have fun and get the most out of being alive. It is much easier to do this when we show up with this open playful attitude.

Chapter 10: Laugh at the Drama

I stood aghast as the wheels of the huge lorry ploughed over the brown leather suitcase, its contents spewing over three lanes of the interstate.

30 years ago we were en route to my eldest brother's wedding celebrations. Driving from the airport to upstate New York, most of my family crammed into the large rented estate car for the beginning of our American adventure.

Facing the rear window in the rear seats of the people carrier with my granddad, I watched as one perfectly balanced suitcase after another slipped from the top of the car into the wide lanes of oncoming traffic.

Our presents, dresses, tuxedos, and our most intimate items were on display to all and sundry as one lorry after another ran over them.

My dad pulled the car over and we stood helplessly and in shock on the hard shoulder, waiting for some kind of divine intervention. Incredibly, one man came to help my dad and risked life and limb to help us retrieve our belongings before the police arrived to close the road.

This was just the beginning.

On the night of the suitcase incident we settled into our hotel rooms, exhausted with jet-lag, only to be awoken two hours later by the sound of fire engines. We spent two hours standing around in our night wear, only to be told it had been a false alarm.

My parents had spent months planning their dream road trip to drive down the east coast of the United States in a camper van for three weeks.

With the wedding behind us and the rest of the family packed off back home, the four of us headed off on the open road – until the camper van broke down ten miles later. After a few hours, it was fixed and sorted and we set off only to break down again a few hours later. This would soon be the pattern as the van broke down everywhere and our adventure included visiting some of the best mechanics in the United States! As we entered Florida my father pulled up at a stop sign to be met with a wave of water over his feet; the shower had burst and water had flooded the inside of the van.

I have no memory of my parents being angry or disappointed because the reality of our trip had not measured up to their dream. Instead all I remember is how much we all laughed at the ridiculousness of it all. We've certainly dined out on this story since!

This attitude has been one of the greatest gifts my parents have instilled in me and it has helped us all weather some of life's greatest dramas, such as redundancies, cancer, deaths, life-threatening accidents and many more. Our family humour can be black, dry, quick and silly, but, above all, we all love telling a good story. Laughing at yourself and life can help you find the way through difficulties and it's an essential companion in travelling.

After a serious sporting accident in my early twenties, I was in a wheelchair for four months and my mum had to help push me around. During our first outing into the city, we got stuck in the bus doorway and she promptly tipped me face-first onto the pavement, having completely misjudged the curb.

We choose how to respond, behave and cope with life. At that moment I could have felt horrified, embarrassed, angry or unloved but instead, I remember laughing so much that I wet myself as she struggled to help pick me up, as she was laughing so much too. It was good medicine after a traumatic time.

The memories of all these times can still bring great joy to us even through our ups and downs and the mistakes we make along the way; we always come back together as a family, because of our capacity to find humour.

Life, as with all good adventures, will have moments that excite, challenge, scare and surprise us. I've found that most of the time seeing the humour in situations and most of all not taking myself too seriously has got me a long way; but sometimes I need reminding...

Chapter 11: Get Out Of Your Head

Standing at the top of the freshly bashed red piste of new power with the sun shining in Austria looking out over the perfect mountain conditions. Yet I felt overwhelmed with anxiety.

I was staying with the friend who was doing the ski season. We had headed out that day with a group of her friends who were seasoned snowboarders. There was nothing wrong with my environment, the snow was fresh and pisted. The equipment was made for me and fit like a glove. I was fit and healthy. However I was the problem. I had not snowboarded for a couple of years and this was day two on the piste. I was still a bit rusty and I now was quickly being pushed out of my comfort zone and doubting my capability. I was ready in body, but not in mind.

My head began to get fuzzy and clouded, as I set off down the mountain. I couldn't get my body to do what I wanted it to. My turns were awkward with no flow or pace to my movements and I was holding back.

My mind and body were out of sync and I was getting more and more frustrated with myself. I knew I could board better than this, but I was afraid I would be left behind or worse still hold the group back, because I wasn't good enough. So when we stopped I began having a little argument with myself, which was quickly interrupted by new friend who gave me the answer to my problem.

"It's not your mind that will get you down here; it's your body, so trust that your body knows what to do!"

She was so right. I had to get out of my mind and into my body and let it drive. I had skills and experience under my belt, yet I was just not trusting my body that it had the muscle memory to respond.

This moment comes to us all, many times in our lives when we have done the practice, got the skills and then all that is left is to trust ourselves. Trust we've got this…

I have never forgotten this advice or this moment as I develop an area of my life and move out of my comfort zone.

A year later I went snowboarding again, but this time with 42 people I didn't know and had one of the best rides of my life - I was balanced, relaxed, in flow, fast and with style. The conditions were perfect and I felt confident in my body, relaxed in my mind and in that moment everything came together and it felt so good.

Chapter 12: All That Glitters is Not Gold

During one of my travels, I visited a famous diamond factory and had the pleasure of briefly wearing a yellow diamond ring, one of the rarest forms in the world. I am mesmerised by diamonds for the way they refract light. Natural, strong and created through pressure and heat, over millions of years of buried 200,000 km below the earth's surface, their journey of coming into form makes them truly precious and their beauty never-ending.

Throughout my 20s, opportunities for luxury kept landing at my feet. I regularly stayed in five-star hotels, mixed with celebrities, Olympians, aristocracy and royalty. Invitations rolled in for season events such as polo and tennis, private estate parties and ambassador's garden parties. At one point I was being gifted so many bottles of Veuve Clicquot and other luxury items that I had a large wooden trunk full, even though I was giving to friends at every opportunity.

I was paid to spend an extended amount of time based in San Francisco with a stunning apartment over looking the city and a white Mustang convertible to drive to our San Jose office. It was the time of the dot.com bubble and, although I was there to work, the work seemed like play. I attended millionaire's balls, partied with new friends, went sightseeing and fell in love with the city.

I felt young, confident and beautiful and there seemed an endless supply of entertainment. I had a lot of fun during those years, but slowly I discovered I was unsatisfied. Each thing was shiny, exciting and new, but still I was left wanting more of something I could not grasp. I began to get bored and restless and the material lifestyle no longer seemed fun. I felt a deep lack of connection, so I walked away to find what that 'more' was…

Many years later, during my road trip around Italy and the northern peak of Lake Como, I came across a beach of black sand and glittering water. As I swam my skin sparkled as though I was swimming through billions of tiny diamonds. It was truly magical but they were not real. The cause of this phenomenon is pyrite, a compound mixture of iron and sulphur — more commonly known as Fool's Gold!

Some things, opportunities and people have the greatest sparkle, without the substance to back up the glitter. Deciphering the difference is part of the journey from fool to wisdom during our lives. We can and should still enjoy the sparkle as long as we are not fooled by its perceived value. I had to search for the sparkle and substance within myself, and understand what I needed to feel satisfied in my life before I could once again enjoy luxury for what it is.

Both nature's beauty and material luxury do not last in the memory if they don't connect with the heart. Our most precious experiences are only remembered and satisfy our soul, because they resonate emotionally and even more deeply if we share them with others who feel the experience too.

Once we know real substance and possess it within, then the shimmering sparkle of luxury and riches in whatever form that attracts you can bring a lot of fun, be embraced and thoroughly enjoyed; knowing it can never be mistaken for what is truly precious.

Even the most stunning priceless diamond is worth nothing without someone who can appreciate how the light shines through it.

Chapter 13: Beyond Control

Italy's Lake Como sits in a bowl surrounded by lush green mountains. The particular area I was in, Abbadia Lariana, is on the west side. My residence was up a hill and overlooking the lake and mountains. During my stay the heat began to rise to extreme temperatures, so much so that all I could do was lie naked on my bed with the fan pointed in my direction, and take intermittent dips in the lake or cold showers. The storm that was brewing became palpable.

The next day after an early morning swim in the Lake, I sat on my balcony for breakfast, thankful for the spitting of rain, that brought with it the hope of release from the intense air pressure. Then unexpectedly the presence of the storm arrived before it did. Although there were no dark clouds to see, every hair on my body became alert, and my instinct told me to turn my head to the right. I was greeted by a dark monster looming towards me. The clouds had descended into the bowl and were now travelling sideways and headed in my direction.

I dived inside only just managing to lock the glass doors before it prowled past. It's power left me in awe. The clouds crackled, the wind racked the whole building, and rain pounded the windows for ten minutes. The noise was deafening – it was like being sat in car wash. Then, as suddenly as it had arrived, it seemed to disappear, leaving a deathly silence. Waiting a few minutes I then tentatively opened the doors. It was clear but the mountain opposite was on now fire, having been struck by lightening.

Although it looked deceiving with blue skies and sunshine, I felt like I was inside a bubble, waiting for it to burst. This was the eye of the storm and soon enough, the second half of the storm came whirling through the bowl of the Lake.

There are forces in the world so much bigger than us and respecting that and our instinct for a response can take us a long way. I always think of this moment when my life is going through a period of change and how it can take on a force of its own or when there are experiences that are beyond my control. Sometimes we must take refuge somewhere safe until the chaos and potential harm passes and the way forward is clearer. However in other moments, it's best to let go, enjoy the experience and marvel at what is occurring.

A few weeks later, during the same trip, I was staying at the most northern tip of the Lake, half way up a mountain. On my first evening, there was a huge electrical storm and I felt intensely drawn to be immersed in it.

I stepped outside of my cabin in the middle of the hillside, outstretched my arms, and danced around barefoot as the warm rain came down. The lightening flickered around the sky, creating illuminations and the thunder clapped at its beauty. I felt truly alive, wild and free to my core.

The next morning as I walked out with my cup of coffee into the field and looked over the Lake, the air felt almost post-coital, as though the masculine and feminine energy of the world had a night of wild passion and now all was well and calm with the world. There's much to be said for that!

JO WARWICK

Chapter 14: The Mountain

I would never have described myself as a mountain goat. I liked to snowboard down mountains, not climb them, then I changed…

From curiosity to climbing up a peak became a building attraction as I got higher and wanted to see more. The experience became intoxicating as the air cleared, the sound quietened, the space expanded, the perspective widened and my mind and body lapped up the challenges.

The transformation happened during my first exploration of the Peak District in Derbyshire and Cheshire, and then the Lake District in Cumbria. I have gazed upon mountains around the world. I have driven up, through and around them. Taken chair lifts to the top and flown over them. Their magnitude and wildness has always appealed to me but I had never hiked them. My hiking had always been about walking off somewhere, not up. Then my first mountain found me and I had to find myself.

Often in life, an opportunity finds us before we think we are ready because it's really a chance to grow through the experience and into what is ahead of us.

It was already a warm summer's morning as I set out for a comfortable hike for a few hours. I had supplies of water and sun cream but, in my naivety, I was ill-prepared for a longer hike than planned. After 90 minutes, I stared at the map, confused how I now found myself on the wrong side of the valley. I soon managed to track down a local farmer who had armed me with casual directions consisting of "up there, fork right when you get to here, and it's clear from there." So I set off back up the mountain I had skirted the edge of with no comprehension of the distance and the heights I was now heading towards.

I continued hiking up for hours, believing it couldn't be that much further until I reached the "fork right when you get to here". With the sun now blazing and phone signal long gone, I was seriously beginning to consider turning around, but instead I choose to carry on, having come this far.

After another hour I reached the brow and found myself on a wide expanse of fenland, overlooking blue sky and the green and brown tops of the surrounding hills and mountains and surrounded by miles and miles of grass and the odd sheep and the map seemed to hold no clues.

The fen having been drenched from a recent downpour became boggier and boggier and it was in those next two hours that I truly met my mountain – of fear. Little demons popped up over and over, until I came face to face with my devil. My devil whispered lies that I was weak and foolish and I would never find my way back. That Faith and I would get stuck here and die. I had been walking for five hours. I was tired, hungry and my legs ached. I'd had enough and I wanted to quit. I was scared and longed to be somewhere safe and dry, yet I was here and turning back was no longer an option. I just had to push on, one step at a time.

As I write this I realise how much this echoed an emotionally dark and painful time of my life when I felt like I was in hell. I knew then too that the only way out of hell is to keep moving forward.

I navigated my way across the seemingly endless fen with intuition, the guide lines from sheep tracks, the lay of the landscape and with a huge heap of faith. As time passed I gradually began to notice a descent and then a new wooden gate appeared. I felt such a rush of hope and excitement as this was the first sign of humanity since the farmer five hours before, so civilisation couldn't be too far away.

The gate lead to a forest road which paved the way back through the valley and, ninety minutes later, I was back at my campsite. Eight hours since I'd set off, I returned a stronger, more confident and capable woman, having conquered my mountain.

I was hooked after that. I became wiser, better prepared and, as my skills improved, I wanted more. Every mountain is different but the experience of peace, satisfaction, challenge, and elevation is hypnotic. There are bigger mountains waiting for me to explore but I have my limits too. I cannot see myself climbing Everest but who knows, things change.

I reflect on this experience when I want to quit in my life and back track to my knowing of my comfort zone, or feel too tired to keep going, because it seems too hard. To remind myself to have determination and belief to keep going and aim higher. To step into those opportunities in life that require bravery, curiosity and adventure.

It's not about choosing difficulty and struggle. Yet sometimes we need to dig deep within and persevere to face a challenge head on, because what we get out of that perseverance, when we know it is for the right cause, is worth so much more than the mountain it may feel like to climb.

Chapter 15: A Higher Perspective

One of the greatest things I've gained from travelling is the capacity to adapt to not just a new perspective, but a higher perspective. To step out of what is in front of me in the present when I begin to get bogged down in the chaos, frustrations, or boredom of day-to-day life.

Those days in South Africa gave me a complete elevation in perspective with the endless plains of flat red soil, blue skies, and the sparsely scattered wildlife and trees.

At sunset, I would watch the sun as it hovered just above the horizon like a giant blazing orange fire ball and then plummet out of sight every evening, only to rise up with the same speed at dawn. Whilst at night, I would lie on the ground in awe of the stars of the Milky Way, which were so clear and bright I felt I could almost reach out and touch them.

My attraction to looking up meant I jumped at the chance to climb into a small two man helicopter which was used for tracking and driving wild game, like a sheep dog in the sky. It was hardly any bigger than a toy and we rose up and shot across the sky with such speed, with nothing weighing us down, open to the elements unconfined by side doors; it was like being in an open top race car!

As we flew above the strolling elephant herds, wildebeest running in their masses, giraffes grazing the tops of the acacia trees, I felt like I was filming a David Attenborough documentary. I had seen these animals and many more up close, individually and in small numbers, but from this distance I could see their strength in numbers, how they lived without human intervention and what it means to be truly wild and free.

When we rise to a higher perspective, life becomes unhindered by the clutter, and we can see our strengths and how we resist, where we are focusing our attention and what we can do to thrive. Above all, it's easier to let go of all the stresses and minutia because we can surrender to the larger forces and allow life to unfold without our need to try to control it.

There is a time to get stuck in and make a stand or take action for change, but it is also essential to be able to step back, rise above the fray and see the bigger picture and the beauty and wonder in its magnitude.

Chapter 16: Trusting All Is Well

With my house rented out and my car stocked to the brim ready for all eventualities, my dog Faith and I arrived at our first campsite in France. Only an hour outside Paris, this was the first step in my road trip across Europe. We were welcomed by beautiful, hot summer weather, and wide-open spaces.

I set up the tent and headed off to the local supermarket to stock up. As I sat in the car park adjusting the windows for Faith who was in the back of the car, my passenger front window suddenly collapsed into the door frame. The window motor had broken and the glass had disappeared. My whole life was in this car, but with nothing to be done but to trust, I headed into the store.

Thankfully the skies were clear that evening. The following morning, I bravely navigated my way to a Volkswagen garage in the industrial side of central Paris. If you have ever driven in Paris you will understand that is a whole adventure in its self. However I was met with delays due to lunch.

My car still packed with most of my belongings sat exposed on the forecourt for 90 minutes. As Faith and I, armed with more trust, headed off to the local café to get some respite from the heat.

Once we returned to the garage I clearly explained the problem using the international language of hand gestures, pointing and interesting face-pulling combined with terrible school girl French – I am convinced at one point I told them my car had a headache. My window was then removed from the door and carefully fixed back in place with nothing more than a piece of cardboard, and that is how it stayed for the next four months as we continued to travel around Europe.

Forced to trust the world with everything I possessed, there was nothing to be done but accept the situation. Once I did, all was well and I even forgot about the strategic cardboard after a while. Travelling has repeatedly shown me that trust is the essential ingredient to life. Trusting that I will find somewhere to sleep; that I can find the right people to connect with; that I will be safe; that I can cope with anything; that I can find a solution to whatever I need.

Things have only gone awry and got bumpy when I get stressed and caught up in fear and there are some examples in this book. From experience I have learned that stepping out into the world with trust in yourself and life attracts trust. Trust gives an air of confidence to other people and there is nothing more attractive to opportunities in life, and nothing less attractive to life's 'predators'.

I'm not always confident and brave but we can only expand out of fear, to do more and be more. So when I want to shrink I step forward and take action with a belief in trust, because I've found that everything does have the tendency to work out perfectly if not only do you believe it will, but more importantly when you let it.

JO WARWICK

Chapter 17: The Turbulence Of Transitions

Travelling is a continual transition from the familiar to the unfamiliar, and can feel turbulent. Just like being on an airplane, we can get battered around if we are not strapped safely into our seats.

An ex-boyfriend of mine shared some great advice from his experience of being in the army where he had to change jobs and locations every two years. "It takes three days, three weeks, three months to adjust to the phases of any transition – three days to feel OK and more settled, three weeks to feel in a state of familiarity and three months to feel comfortable and confident." I've kept this is mind ever since.

On any new adventure, the first week is always the worst. It can bring the most intense mixture of emotions. I've found that after the initial high of setting off, the first three days can be a little irritating as my body and mind struggles to unwind and resists being in the moment; it wants to create plans and control things. *How am I going to do this? What am I going to do? How will I spend my time?* I begin to fall into a strange sense of boredom. *"How will live like this for the next however many months?"*

All of these feelings are really a fear of the unknown. I have learned what helps me get through the first three turbulent weeks, as it stops feeling like a holiday and becomes a new way of life. Like being safety-belted onto the seat, I need some routine and structure – even if that means daily routines like showers, shopping etc. I've found going to the supermarket helps me feel more settled.

However, like the plane, I also need to keep moving through it so I've found it's best to keep active – if you lie around, your mind will get you! Lots of walking and exploring has helped me with this, so that I am physically tired which helps me sleep really well and start to naturally unwind and slow down – every day needs to have a mini adventure!

I've noticed I have to be aware that I need different things at different times during the whole experience, because both the world and I keep changing. Sometimes those things are truly practical and for me often the hardest to see when having an adventure…

Only a couple of weeks into my last big adventure, I'd spent 24 hours in a tent with no sign of the torrential rain clearing, and came to the decision I needed to go find a camping store and buy something bigger.

My last tent had done me well, traveling around Europe, as well as many short trips in between. Although it was a three-man tent, it seemed to shrink in size with me, a wet dog and the heavy rain. Dashing to-and-from the car to get things added extra stress, which is something I never want during the transition phase.

In the end I purchased a swanky five-man tent and it was like moving house from a studio flat to a two bedroom bungalow! It seemed weird at first because we had so much room, but I felt prepared for all weathers for the next three to four months of wandering around the UK, as it moved from summer into autumn.

As I gradually meandered northwards, the weather became colder so my next investment was thermals. They didn't quite cut it, so soon after it was a new sleeping bag. The camping specialist enquired how long I had owned and used my current sleeping bag and I proudly announced that it had been around the world with me and I had been using it for 12 years. He couldn't stop laughing, saying that no wonder it wasn't keeping me warm anymore. It was time to invest in a new one, and oh my did I sleep toasty and warm that night!

Riding out the turbulence in life as we journey into new jobs, relationships, houses and world explorations, requires a conscious attention to achieving balance. Balance between our inner flexibility to change and the right practical tools in the here and now to feel secure day to day, until the turbulence passes and we discover we have transitioned as smoothly as possible into calm, clear skies and warm sunny days.

Chapter 18: High With Joy

I have always had a longing to be high up in the sky, and above all be able to fly. I live by the sea and spend a lot of time enviously watching the seagulls playing on the wind thermals, and often, when it gets windy, I stand on the headland with my arms outstretched imagining the feeling of flying.

I have tried to capture the feeling of flying through zip-lining, flying microlights and gliders, paragliding, riding in helicopters, as well as normal planes of course. I'm sure I was a bird in a former life – I've got the bug for feeling free with my wings open. As amazing as all these experiences were, they have never come close to what I imagine it's really like.

I wanted the real deal, to fly as me in my body, but skydiving had never appealed as it's falling not flying in its true sense – it's not off the cards yet but I want to go up, rather than just down! Luckily, I discovered indoor skydiving and honestly, I cannot recommend it enough.

As we entered the air-locked tunnel, I was a bundle of excitement and nerves. I stepped across the doorway into the wind tunnel, held hands with the instructor and was elevated until I was completely horizontal to the ground and six feet off the safety net! The instructor lined me up with the wind jets and let go of me as they turned up the wind pressure to 160mph. With my arms outstretched and head up, I was flying - really flying!

After a while the instructor grabbed one of my hands and feet and began to spin me until we headed up to the top of the wind tunnel just like Charlie in Willy Wonka and the Chocolate Factory. Then it happened.

The wind pressure fell away, the world became full of peace, and I was in heaven. The higher I went, the happier I became and I didn't want to come down – but what goes up and all that. We swooped down like birds and then catching the wind pressure up again we went. I felt the joy fill my whole being. With each swoop and elevation, I felt complete surrender, as though it was the most natural thing in the world.

I knew as a child and rediscovered through travelling, that the clearer my mind the higher I feel in my body and soul, the happier I am, and that this is the best way to get the most enjoyment out of my life. So everyday I practice owning my internal wings and if my thoughts and feelings begin to come down to a lower vibe of fear I take control and seek to swoop back up as quickly as possible, by getting back in alignment with life's wind jets (Love) and focusing on where I want to be; flying high feeling good — happy, joyful, peaceful, satisfied and free.

You can find out more about aligning and owning your inner wings in The Big Book Of Love...

.

Chapter 19: A Journey of Food

In so many ways my life has been a journey of food and it is travelling that has opened up a world of opportunity to access incredible flavours, spices, textures, colours and passion all wrapped up in the wonderful act of eating.

I always enjoy visiting foreign supermarkets to explore the differences, but I adore getting lost in a fresh food market. I will seek out these moments of heaven with the bright colours, intoxicating smells, where you are encouraged to touch, pick up, really have a good look at and taste. The sound of the babbling foreign market traders and customers are like music to my ears.

I am a foodie. I love to cook, feed other people and above all I love to eat. Yet it hasn't always been this way. I've been so poor in my life that I lived on 'tuna splat' as I called it; dry pasta, tin tomatoes and sometimes with or without tin tuna. I've scavenged, I've lived off the land, I've gone without, but I've also experienced an abundance of choice and eaten fine dining. I have eaten things I adored and tried things I discovered I didn't like, and definitely eaten things I would never eat again.

For a large period of my life I had a strange and twisted relationship with food often hinged on guilt and fear, where I could not really see its value, let alone allow my passion and love for it. It was my time in South Africa that began to completely alter this sad and lacking perspective.

The local guys who worked for the'Afrikaans' farms at that time would leave their families, travel far and for periods of time come to earn money to take back. They slept under the stars and lived on predominately on maize porridge which is cheap and gives an amount of substance and sustenance; unless fresh meat becomes available.

One day on the trip I had to assist in putting a small, stocky antelope out of it's suffering after being injured by the antler of another. It was my first and only time I've physically killed an animal. Although having lived on farms and being involved in horses for a large part of my life I have been witness to a few. The experience was humbling and it was the only decision, out of love and respect for the animal.

I then forced myself to watch the twelve local guys who assisted the conversation team, to butcher it with such swift skilled care, that in five minutes there was nothing to waste. They all had fresh meat to eat. The hide was used for warmth. Then the carcass was left for the wild scavengers who gathered quickly, drawn by the smell, to finish it off. It wasn't pleasant but it made sense. It felt real unlike the sterilised packaging in the supermarket which enables complete emotional and mental detachment.

This experience finally taught me to have respect for food, for what I eat and to eat with appreciation. I learnt to eat with my eyes, my nose, my tastebuds, my mind and with my touch. Only with this shift to food consciousness did I begin to make not only better choices about how, what and when I eat. Over time my perspective towards food became abundant and pleasurable, so much so that eating and good food grew to be a source of great excitement for me where ever I am in the world.

JO WARWICK

Chapter 20: When It's Right

This chapter is not about the literal experience of travelling, but finding our right way of travelling through life.

For my 40th birthday I was gifted a day of driving a Ferrari around Silverstone Circuit – nine laps, 20 miles and a hot lap with a professional. I have always been proud of the fact I am a good driver and I love driving, but this was taking it to a new level. I have driven a variety of cars: some sports cars, some old bangers, as well as tractors and an HGV horsebox for many years. One of the ways I love to see other countries is through road trips; I love the feel of exploring new territory with the sun shining, the windows open and some tunes to sing along to.

I was unbelievably excited beforehand, but when I stepped into the practice car for my five test runs to help me adjust to the two mile race track, I have never been so afraid! The practice car was a pimped-up Toyota GTI and I was pushed way beyond my comfort zone as the instructor who was pushy and hectic in his manner guided me to drive in a way that was totally counter-intuitive.

I was repeatedly told not to brake as I came towards bends, drive fast into the corners, maintain confidence and speed through the bends, and accelerate out of them. In theory this sounded fine. In practice however at speed, with the other cars on the race track and in a car which felt really wrong to me I was so scared that I felt my insides go squiffy with intense fear. Instead of slowing down or getting out of the car, which I felt desperate to do at one point, I had to put my foot down on the accelerator and keep going. Although I did not trust my instructor he didn't let me chicken out – he even gave me an A+ for my prolific swearing!

When I got back to the starting depot I was shaking, my confidence on the floor and I hadn't even driven the Ferrari yet. I went for a pee and on my return, my dad gave me a big hug and told me to "Man up and go drive that Ferrari"as he pushed me towards the car.

I was to be completely surprised. I settled into the Ferrari and felt all the tension fall away. Although the Toyota was only 200 BHP, compared to the Ferrari which is nearly 500 BHP it is lower to the ground, it sticks to the road and glides around bends. It felt so powerful and a dream to drive with its paddle gears and no clutch, that I felt no fear and only desire to go faster. It was my right tool for the job in hand and my confidence soared, proved by me reaching over 120mph on the Grand Prix straight and 80mph on a hairpin bend!

My Ferrari instructor was calm, clear and complimentary, awarding me an A+ for my driving skills. He said I was smooth, fast, consistent and a great driver who needed little tuition – My four laps in the Ferrari went by with such pleasure and ease that I could have driven that car all day long. I felt like I belonged and was high on adrenaline when I got out.

I remember this contrast of experience often and it highlights so clearly the difference it makes when we trust our instinct and choose the right fit for who we are, no matter if its during global travels or in our careers, relationships, houses etc. Many times in the past I have moved towards what feels wrong to me and just like the being in the Toyota I began to lose all confidence, slow down and got more and more upset, until I could stop and get out of the situation. Those wrong moments though helped me to know what is right for me. So that through my travels and along my journey I have learnt to really trust the innate emotional guidance system within us all. So that I do my best to move towards and choose only what feels right — and like getting into the Ferrari all fear melts away, and I begin to move forward in pure pleasure, relaxed and enjoying every minute and absolutely wanting more.

JO WARWICK

Chapter 21: Dance Me To The End Of Life

Dance has been a large part of my travels. Music, especially live, enables me to get my groove on and be joyful. It has facilitated my connection with so many people around the world in a way that verbal communication never could. I have danced with people, young and old, in kitchens, sitting rooms, city streets, bars, nightclubs, posh restaurants, in the bush, in fields, on beaches, in tents, at daytime and at night.

Although we may engage in dancing with other people, like sex, travelling and life, we are always truly dancing alone. Dancing is a conversation between our soul and the rhythm, vibration and feel of the music. It is a physical expression of our inner self: our desires, fascinations, curiosities and rhythm through form and personal presentation.

Towards the end of one of my trips I stopped in at the city of Bristol. It was a sunny Sunday afternoon and I came across two guys dancing solo in the middle of the park. It was an impromptu outdoor silent disco and anyone could join in. People walked on by, staring as these guys surrendered to the music in their headphones and full out doing their thing. I watched their joy of expression with longing, but my anxiety held me back.

Holding myself back isn't something I would do when I'm travelling; I follow what feels good - or in the iconic words of Joseph Campbell I " *follow my bliss*" I had become disconnected from true myself and makes me happy, so I felt inhibited and then frustrated by my sudden awareness.

Two months later on the streets of Barcelona, a local salsa band began playing, as the sun shone and a party started. As soon as the first few people began dancing and I leaped up to get involved. Soon enough I was dancing with an older Spanish man and, although we didn't dance well as a couple and our bodies end up in a tangled mess, we laughed and laughed and laughed. We were not stylish but we had a lot of fun.

All shared life experiences are a dance in some form. They can be brief or lasting. They can be playful or passionate; an instant match or total lack of harmony. As we relax, focus on how we feel, surrender to being in the moment and get comfortable with each other, the energetic dance that happens between you becomes alive and electric.

It is that energy of life which flows through us and connects us with the world around us and with other people, which is our greatest dance partner of all. We can choose to be in or out of sync, speed up or slow down with it. However once we learn to dance in harmony with it, and be the best partner we can by listening to each impulse and direction, we can fully let go and dance our way through life to the rhythm of our own music.

JO WARWICK

Chapter 22: Travelling Home

Through travelling, I discovered how to live in a state of harmony, in flow with a deep trust in life, so things unfold with more ease, wonder and joy, even when I am challenging myself. I feel relaxed and at home within myself and in love who I'm being and where I am.

Sometimes my global travel has been an act of running away, as well as getting away. It has been a running to, as well as a stroll or leap into the unknown. I've travelled to discover the new, but also the old and familiar. I travelled to explore the wider world, but also to find home.

For all the amazing places that have tempted me, I never felt a strong enough desire to stay and so every time I would return to the UK. Then I would begin to lose my sense of self and fall into a negative mentality, thinking that life is hard work and I must prove my worth to receive any rewards. My faith and trust would dampen and my joy would seep away.

Travelling has been a journey of becoming myself over and over, but for a long time losing myself if I stopped. I was determined to learn how I could live fully as I do when travelling while having a physical place I could call home.

I am my home. The world is also my home, and I had a need for a more intimate place that I could return to over and over, which resonated with who I truly am during my travels.

In my late 20s, I visited Newquay in Cornwall with a friend to try surfing. I fell head over heels in love with the place. It was an intense attraction, so I began to visit over and over again, driving between five and ten hours each way. I fell for the adventure of surfing, the playful attitude and partying with live music and handsome healthy looking boys. I felt young and alive and began to make friends who lived there.

Every time I left, it became more and more painful and I would grieve for the next few days as I returned to what seemed in so many ways my incredible life in Cambridge, where I commuted to London. My job was organising sporting events around the world, and I'd get to mix with celebrities and Olympians, stay in five star hotels, be given luxury items and surrounded by so-called successful men.

However all I wanted was to be back in Newquay, close to the sea, with salt in my hair, walking in flip flops and hanging out with people who were relaxed, open and sociable. Then, as the initial attraction to Newquay and the lifestyle settled down, it became clear that I was drawn to the ocean, the space and colour of the Cornish landscape, and the pace of life and between both of these I felt joy. I had found my home.

Through my travels, I have discovered core themes and elements that I am consistently attracted to, no matter where I go in the world.

- Vibrant colour – I look for this in landscapes, people, attitudes, and food
- Connection – in animals and nature, as well lovers and friends, new and old, who made me feel closer to love and my faith, than further away
- Adventure and challenge – I thrive on opportunities for growth
- Rhythm - I have a love of music, but I also discovered my need to be in my own personal rhythm, which is the essence of travelling alone
- Texture and flavour – This can only be experienced through touch, taste and being present in the moment.

Although my trips to Newquay became more and more frequent, it still took me two years to finally make the leap, as I tried to figure out if I could live in Cornwall and keep my job. I was unsure if I could break out of my old life, but in the end my hand was forced by my job. So I left my Cambridge life for a new adventure and trusted it would all work out. Everyone from my old city life told me I was mad and too young to be getting out, but I had a bit of money and I rented out my flat, brought a tent and drove down. I lived in that three-man tent for three months.

I took time out and immersed myself in surfing twice a day and waitressing to meet people. Slowly things unfolded and I discovered a new life. As I relaxed I was inspired by a new career and went on to study again. A year later, after a caravan and then a house share, I fell in love with an 18th Century Cornish cottage. I went on to adore it for 10 years, and shared it with housemates and then with Airbnb guests who came from all over Europe to stay, bringing the essence of travelling to me.

This relationship with my home was not all peace and love as I changed and fell in and out of losing 'travelling me' and then finding myself again. When I felt my physical home of Newquay wasn't changing and growing, I felt stifled. However, each time I left for an adventure I would always feel the pull to return.

I got stronger in my ability to trust myself and translated my travelling skills to my life at home. I learned to stay aligned with my true self and the flow of love, as I describe in my first book, The Big Book of Love – just like the baggage we take as we travel through life, some things are essential. For me, home is within me, but it is also a place that calls to my soul that feels right. It cannot satisfy every part of my life but the joy of home is that, over time, we explore somewhere new and then return to appreciating it with fresh eyes.

My home starts with my inner divine connection, knowing who I am and my physical home then resonating with me. I did sell my cottage two years ago because the love affair had come to an end. Now, I live overlooking the beach with vast windows, so I have a sense of being outside all the time. I see vibrant colour every day from the sea, beach, coastline and sky, as well as in the wild and stunning garden. I live on a headland with the beach on one side and surrounded by hills, trees, fields and a river on the other. The space and freedom this brings me gives me so much joy.

I have love and connection with old friends and new like-minded people with whom I have real open relationships with and add fun and meaning to my life – as well as my dog Faith of course.

I live at my own rhythm every day which suits me in the way I work, rest and play and am most productive and connected.

I have texture and flavour in my life through regular dancing, cooking, dining, sharing with others and being in love.

The adventure is added with live gigs, festivals, comedy shows, and theatre, short walking trips, and wider travel. I no longer feel the need to run away and I enjoy returning home as much as going, because I no longer lose myself in the transition.

Through my travels around the world, I found my home both within, but also surrounding me – the place that resonates and reflects the true me. I do my best to keep living what I've learnt and share. Appreciating and truly enjoying what is in front of me in the present, as well listening to my desire for what is coming next, because all of this is part of the biggest travelling adventure of all: LIFE.

Other Books By Jo Warwick

The Big Book Of Love

Loving Yourself, Dating With Love, Loving Relationships

The Big Book Of Love is a guidebook to living successfully in flow with love and the Law Of Attraction. Designed to help you understand how love works and remember you are love at your core. Empowering you, whether male or female, with the skills and tools to make practical love-based decisions for your greatest well-being and happiness, and guide you towards truly intimate, lasting relationships.

Love Psychologist Jo Warwick has since 2006 helped thousands of men and women around the world to understand and embrace love abundantly, and now she's combined her life's work and personal experience to create The Big Book Of Love.

Available to buy from Amazon and other retailers...

Printed in Poland
by Amazon Fulfillment
Poland Sp. z o.o., Wrocław